I AM

Intentional!

I AM
Intentional!

Living Life
Purposely and *Unapologetically*

Adecia L. Spain, M.Ed.

I AM *Intentional!*

Copyright © 2022 by Adecia L. Spain, M.Ed.

All rights reserved. No part of this publication may be reproduced, distributed, or transmitted in any form or by any means, including photocopying, recording, or other electronic or mechanical methods, without the prior written permission of the publisher.

ISBN-13: 979-8-9864061-0-7

Unless otherwise indicated, all Scripture quotations are from the New King James Version®. Copyright © 1982 by Thomas Nelson. KJV is taken from the King James Version.

Cover design: A Plus Creations

Printed in the United States of America

Dedication

I wish to dedicate this book to the many women in my family who write! Growing up it was the note on the front door telling you to go around, or one on the cabinet doors reminding you to wash your dish. The notes on the refrigerator from my grandmother warned me and my cousins of the consequences of putting pots in there to keep from washing them. The teacher, bus driver, neighbor, no one was exempt, not even exes. Now we have moved on to text, emails, and social media posts. Yes, the legacy of writers continues. Never remain silent or silenced: WRITE!

Before I formed you in the womb *I knew you*; before you were born *I sanctified you*; and *I ordained you* a prophet to the nations Jeremiah 1:5

Contents

Acknowledgments 1

Bless The Lord 3

Fearfully And Wonderfully Made 7

Lord, I Trust You 11

Unapologetically Me 15

All In 19

Endure Difficult Seasons 23

Stay On The Wheel 27

It Takes Work 31

Redeem The Time 35

I Am Not An Island 39

Embrace Differences 43

Handfuls On Purpose 47

Overcome 51

Perfected Peace 55

Live In The Moment 59

Rest	63
Blessed To Be A Blessing	67
Victory In Obedience	71
Ask Big	75
Forgive Early And Often	79
Words Matter	83
Using My Gifts	87
Willing To Be Misunderstood	91
Rejoice	95
Be Selfish	99
What Is In My Hand	103
Chosen	107
God Has Not Changed His Mind About Me	111
Rest And Restoration	115
Love On Purpose	119
Divine Connections	123
About the author	127

Acknowledgments

I took a Creative Writing class at the Xavier University of Louisiana only because it did not interfere with my duties as a student-athlete. What "worked with my schedule" was a divine setup. The class was inspirational and challenging and affirmed my love of writing as an expression of freedom.

God you knew! I am eternally grateful and I thank you for the gift of writing which has enhanced my life and has allowed me to use my gift to bless others.

Inspired…

Bless The Lord

> *Bless the LORD, O my soul: and all that is within me, bless his holy name.* PSALM 103:1 KJV

Psalm 103 is one of many in which King David exalts the LORD. An imperfect man, but one which the Bible declared to be a man after God's own heart. How did David earn such an honor? David pursued God through repentance, prayer, and praise. Are you intentionally blessing the LORD? Are you bestowing upon Him the honor and glory He is due? In Psalm 116:12, the writer has taken inventory of his life and exclaims, "What shall I render unto the LORD for all of His benefits towards me?" He remembers being compassed with troubles, and overcome with sorrow to the degree he felt hell was upon him, yet when he called on the name of the LORD God heard him and delivered him! Hallelujah! After remembering this, David then rejoices and is overcome with gratefulness because of God's grace and mercy towards him.

God is watching to see how we will respond to His goodness. We have called out to Him and in kindness, He has answered. There have been times when we did not call on His name and out of the abundance of His grace and mercy, He knew our need and provided anyway. Yes, He is that type of God!

"I will bless the LORD" is personal! What will you do in remembrance of His continual goodness towards you? Will you offer a sacrifice of praise? Will you rejoice in the LORD always, whether the times or good or bad? The beauty of our God is that there is more than enough to praise Him just for who He is!

All we are and all that we will ever be is because of Him. Someone can see the hand of God on your life and thank God for what He is doing but they are on the outside! They only know in part what He has done but you know the whole story which is why praise is personal. No one knows like you know the magnitude of His grace on your life! Your praise should be rooted in gratefulness of heart, not done systematically or out of duty. I have often heard that what comes from the heart touches the heart. Invest the time as the Psalmist David did and acknowledge God's hands upon your life. When my children acknowledge my sacrifices, it increases my desire to pour out even more upon them. I challenge you to create time to remember your blessings, recognize God's intentionality in blessing you, and then pour out your praise as you rejoice in the goodness of the Lord.

Affirmation

> *"I will bless the LORD at all times; because He is blessing me at all times."*

Fearfully And Wonderfully Made

> *For You formed my inward parts; You covered me in my mother's womb. I will praise You, for I am fearfully and wonderfully made; Marvelous are Your works. And that my soul knows very well.* PSALM 139:13-14 NKJV

Months away from my cousin's 40th birthday, she announces, "I'm pregnant!" Finally, our family's own Supernanny would now be able to pour love into her child after years of selflessly pouring love into and caring for the children of family and friends. As expected, many were shocked, stunned, filled with tears, and overjoyed! Truth be told, we had been secretly awaiting this day and now it was here. Moments of delight shifted from bliss to bridezilla-like baby shower planning. Who would we invite? What would be the perfect color combinations? What place would accommodate all who wanted to celebrate? Would it be a boy or girl or maybe both, because fraternal twins run in our family? The excitement quickly shifted to the concern of perfectly capturing the significance of the event. We were caught up in the moment, making plans for a child who would eventually grace us with his or her presence.

While reflecting on the joy of that moment, I was drawn to Psalm 139, where King David reflected on how intimate and intentional God was in His creation. He boldly proclaimed it was God who formed his inward parts and covered him in his mother's womb; David praised God for fearfully and wonderfully making him just as God did with all the other marvelous works of creation. King David gloried God for seeing him when he was mere substance, and unformed and then taking the time to make him His masterpiece. God uniquely created David and delighted in the awesome plans He would do in and through David's life.

You also are one of the marvelous works of God's hands! You were created with purpose, on purpose, and for purpose. Just as God had plans for every living thing He created, He too has plans for you. You should never feel insignificant or worthless. As you were being fashioned, God was aware of all you would need to live purposely and intentionally and placed everything you would need within you. Now is the time to seek Him and discover those hidden treasures in your earthen vessel. Seek God with your whole heart and you will find Him. And when you seek and find Him, He will begin to reveal to you your greatness and why you exist for such a time as this. That is good news! It is imperative to go to Him and allow Him to define you. Who knows more about getting the optimal performance out of a thing than its Creator?

You are not an accident; neither are you a mistake. From the very beginning, you were uniquely thought of and created: eyes, height, talents, and natural abilities. You were gifted with everything you would need to show forth the glory of God. Never doubt or undervalue your worth. You have been divinely designed, perfect for the people you have been called to serve. Draw near to God and allow Him to reveal His plan and purpose for your life.

Affirmation

"I am fearfully and wonderfully made to show forth God's glory!"

Lord, I Trust You

> *And also the Strength of Israel will not lie nor repent: for he is not a man, that he should repent.* 1 SAMUEL 15:29 KJV

My son did not tell me the truth about something, so as his punishment, he was to list reasons why it was not okay to lie. Once he finished his list, I had him read his responses aloud. One response caught my attention as he read, and I was instantly reminded of precious truth. Through a muffled response, I heard my son say, "it will cause people to lose trust in you." Something about that particular answer hit differently! Through my son's awareness and ownership of his wrongdoing, I was immediately convicted and comforted! Convicted, because I had been mad at God about some doors in my life that remained closed that I felt should have already been opened.

I was comforted because as I pondered my son's response, I could not remember what God had lied to me about. There was not anything He had done that would have caused me to lose trust in Him. I could not think of anything! There were answers to situations that God answered according to His will and not mine but He had not lied to me!

My son's truth hit me strongly because I was in the process of having my mind renewed. I did not have a positive self-identity because all I had heard growing up was what I was not and what I needed to change but never an emphasis on what was right about me.

As I began to seek God I realized so much of what I had believed for years were lies! Lies people told me about me and what I could or could not accomplish. Lies I had told myself, which limited my potential.

Oh, and the countless lies the enemy had convinced me to believe about myself and how God was not interested in me because I was flawed. Those lies had me bound, only scratching the surface of greatness, but never experiencing it in its fullness, the way God had predestined it to be.

Truthfully, it was easier for me to believe the lies I was told than to receive and embrace God's truth about myself. I was not actively pursuing what the Word promised was my inheritance as God's daughter. I knew He desired for me to have His absolute best. I faced the challenge of weighing God's truth versus the ongoing, repeated lies. You know the lies, "you're not worth it," "you're not pretty or smart enough," "you're too old or too young," "you come from this side of town or was born into that family." Despite it all, God's truth prevailed! God proved Himself faithful concerning His promises and He would not start a work that He had no intentions of finishing.

You are so loved by God. It is time to rest on what He said! The wrong mindset hinders and robs you of achieving your fullest potential. It will take work but put your hard hat on and begin to tear down the lies you have believed about yourself which are contrary to God's word. Experiencing an intentional and purposeful life will not happen without getting in the Word of God and learning what His promises are. As you discover these truths, meditate upon them and it will dismantle the lies. Daily confessions of His truths will give you back the ownership of what is rightfully yours as a joint heir with Christ! He who has promised you is Faithful. You can trust in Him.

Affirmation

"I believe God; I choose to stand in His truth regarding me."

Unapologetically Me

> *But by the grace of God I am what I am: and his grace which was bestowed upon me was not in vain; but I labored more abundantly than they all: yet not I, but the grace of God which was with me.* I CORINTHIANS 15:10 KJV

I remember hearing that a friend called me an "educated dummy." I was disappointed because of who said it because I considered her a friend. I did not ask what context it was used or what was the motivation behind her remark. I only shook my head in shock but later that day I decided to take what was said and conduct an honest evaluation of whether I was portraying myself as an "educated dummy." The short answer was, "no," but after careful consideration, and being honest with myself, I had to admit I had been minimizing who I knew I was around others.

Because of a root of rejection, I had a desire to be liked, which led to me never wanting to stand out from the crowd, so I chose to blend in. I chose to be silent and allowed others to silence me because it was easier to go along with what everyone else thought, even when at times I had a different perspective. I would not dare write or speak what I felt out of fear of going against the grain and running people away. I had a Bachelor's and two Master's degrees, and I was in circles where it mattered to many but not to me. I was just Adecia so I could see how that could be perceived as an "educated dummy" because I was not exhibiting what I had.

I have always been appreciative of what God had allowed me to accomplish, yet here I was, downplaying myself, pretending to be something that I was not around others. Because of the fear of rejection, I did not want to come across as prideful. After God convicted me of carrying a false humility that was rooted in insecurity, I decided I would no longer make myself small for anyone. I chose to glorify God in how He had blessed me. Imagine me, six feet tall, thinking I could walk into a room and disappear, and no one would see me? Comical! The Apostle Paul was a very intelligent man. Yet he did not brag or boast in himself, but he declared that "by the grace of God I am who I am." He gave all glory to God for who he was.

Not long after I learned of my friend's comment, we were assigned presentations in my graduate psychology classes.

I challenged myself to not only go first but to do my presentation alone. This was outside of my natural element, but I was putting myself out there, taking the limits off, because I knew I was more than an "educated dummy." My friend was not in the class so it was not to "show her" but I realized I was robbing God by not representing Him well.

By the grace of God, I did amazing! I was prepared and did my absolute best. Using all the resources available to me, I presented and set the bar high. Being unapologetically Adecia challenged my classmates to get a whole new game plan to deliver their presentations. They were pleased with my work and it ignited a fire in them. The Bible tells us that iron sharpens iron. When we are unwavering in who we are called and how we are gifted, it builds, motivates, and encourages others to do likewise.

I challenge you to be great! Do not hide or diminish who you have been created to be. If you ever feel yourself shrinking because of insecurity or not wanting to show how great you are, remember God has called you into that greatness.

Affirmation

"I am unapologetically me and I make no excuses for being who God created."

All In

> Then Jesus said to His disciples, "If anyone desires to come after me, let him deny himself, and take up his cross, and follow Me. For whoever desires to save his life will lose it, but whoever loses his life for My sake will find it.
> MATTHEW 16:24-25 NKJV

I am a member of the ministerial staff at my church. During one of our staff development training, the assignment was to develop a sermon from the Bible verse Matthew 8:22, "But Jesus said unto him, Follow me; and let the dead bury their dead." The scripture dealt with the cost of discipleship and how we should respond when Jesus says, "Follow me?" Obedience! When responding to Jesus's call to follow Him, He expects us to forsake all and immediately obey. In the preceding verses, the one who was called asked Jesus if he could first go and bury his father and then he would follow, to which Jesus responded, "let the dead bury the dead."

Forsaking all was not a new expectation. In the Old Testament, God commanded Abram to get out of his country from his father's house, away from what was familiar to Abram, and into a land that God would show him. Abram obeyed and went without knowing where he was going or how God would establish him. Abram responded in faith by immediately obeying God. His obedience and unwavering faith in God earned him the title of the "Father of the Faith" because he believed in God and it was credited to him as righteousness.

Out immediate and total obedience is also expected when we are called. It is a privilege and honor to be chosen to represent God our creator. Many when called left their families and livelihood to follow Christ! Withholding nothing!

When you are all in, it means every effort is made to allow God to fully work His plan and purpose out in your life. You submit to His will trusting that He knows what is best for you. As you submit to Him, you trust Him to order your steps onto the path where His plan for your life is achieved.

I recall an artist proclaiming yes is the only appropriate answer to the call of Christ. Because of the seriousness of the work that has to be done for The Kingdom's sake, we have to be ALL IN! Being double-minded or lukewarm benefits no one. We have to be trustworthy and dependable. Just as we expect God to hold to His word, we too have to be committed to trusting Him.

Are you all in or is there a Plan B, in case the cost to follow Christ is too hard for you? I eagerly said yes when I came to Christ but became discouraged along the journey. I wanted all the benefits without having to submit. I was willfully ignorant to the things God had to perfect in my character, attitude, and behaviors before I would be able to effectively do what He called me to do integrally.

Your "ALL IN" could be being the best wife or husband or the best mother or father. It could be serving in a leadership position in your profession or a ministry. Whatever it is and wherever He has called you, allow God to use you as light and salt to impact your circle of influence for His glory. Be a willing vessel of love, pouring out to all those in need of what you have been blessed with.

Affirmation

"Father, I am all in! I delight in doing Your will!"

Endure Difficult Seasons

> For I know the thoughts that I think toward you, saith the LORD, thoughts of peace, and not of evil, to give you an expected end. JEREMIAH 29:11 KJV

"This Can't Be God!" I grew up hearing, "if it's good, it's God, and if it's bad, it's the devil." While experiencing what I believed to be then one of the most trying seasons of my life, I knew there was no way God could have allowed it. I was being taken advantage of, intentionally sabotaged, and repeatedly overlooked. I prayed to be removed from the environment and had others praying, but God did not allow me to leave. It was all a part of His plan that I remain there because he was doing work in me through the challenges I faced. I had to remain faithful to my assignments, serve with the right attitude, and forgive the people who had done me wrong. It hurt, and I did not think it was fair, but I was obedient to what God commanded.

That experience reminded me of God's demand on the Israelites whom he had allowed King Nebuchadnezzar to carry away captives from Jerusalem unto Babylon. Yes, God had led His people into captivity. God sent a letter to them by way of the prophet Jeremiah confirming that He ordained that season for their lives. The Israelite's captivity would be for 70 years despite the lying prophets who told them it would be shorter.

In the prophet's letter, God told them to build houses and dwell in them, plant gardens, and eat their fruit. They also had to be fruitful and multiply in the land. It may not have made sense at the time, but it was all a part of God's plan to increase them. The Israelites had to seek peace and also pray for the peace of Babylon. God commanded this because He was more concerned with the attitude of their heart during their trying season. God wants what is good for His people. It is He who determines how to accomplish that good.

Included in Jeremiah's letter was a PROMISE! The Lord assured the Israelites that after 70 years of captivity, He would visit them and perform His good word toward them. They were to be of good cheer because God's thoughts toward them were good and not evil to give them an EXPECTED end, the end they had hoped for. After their obedience in that season, God would forgive them and restore them.

Are you willing to become rooted and grounded in a place that feels like captivity but God has ordained it? Are you willing to find peace in a place and among a people God has chosen without your permission? Would you be obedient and pray for a place and people you consider your enemies?

God never promised only good things would happen to us but He has promised us those things would work out for our good. We will experience some uncomfortable seasons and make personal sacrifices for God's promises to be fulfilled in our lives.

While experiencing any rough seasons, wholeheartedly seek God at all times. He is not hiding from you; you have not been abandoned. While you are going through this, He desires to be the one you seek for comfort and understanding. Because just when you think, "this can't be God," it may very well be.

Affirmation

"I trust the LORD at all times."

Stay On The Wheel

> *Then the word of the LORD came to me, saying: "O house of Israel, can I not do with you as this potter?" says the LORD. "Look, as the clay is in the potter's hand, so are you in My hand, O house of Israel!*
> *JEREMIAH 18:5-6 NKJV*

Process! A series of actions or steps taken to achieve a particular end. The ultimate goal of our relationship with God is to be transformed into the image and likeness of our Savior Jesus Christ. 2 Corinthians 3:18 emphasizes, "But we all, with open face beholding as in a glass the glory of the Lord, are changed into the same image from glory to glory, even as by the Spirit of the Lord."

This spiritual makeover has been regarded by many as "The Process."

As believers in Christ, we reflect the glory of the Lord. In Christ we are new creatures, the old life has gone and the new life has come. As our bodies are submitted to the Holy Spirit, He processes us. The more we know God we understand the necessity of being transformed from glory to glory.

The Word of the Lord came to Prophet Jeremiah to go down to the potter's house to behold the work the potter was doing at his wheel. God sought to show Jeremiah that all was not lost with Israel, and just as the potter was able to rework the marred clay, He would do the same with Israel if they would submit to Him. The potter's work on the wheel is a process. I attended a pottery class, and I remember sitting still at the wheel, paying close attention to the instructor. I had to be patient as I worked the clay on the wheel. It was best to have my desired result in mind because it guided me in shaping the clay. The clay did not offer any resistance, it yielded to me its potter.

Reflecting on the experience, every step was necessary, and compromising on any of them would have ruined my creation when it got to the firing stage. It would not have been able to withstand the intense pressure. As with the clay, so it is with us. We must stay on the wheel and allow

God, the Master Potter, to work out the imperfections in us. Pruning our character, integrity, attitudes, and motives is needed to honorably serve as the vessel God envisioned. Just as God knew Jeremiah was a prophet before He formed him in his mother's womb, God knows His plans for you. As you submit, you are coming into agreement with what has already been ordained and God can finish His work.

Today, I am grateful for The Process! I once listened to others say how hard the wheel was for them and I delayed getting on for myself. But now, in the potter's hands, this transformation on the wheel has been the most rewarding experience ever! It has not always felt good, but it has produced greatness.

I encourage you to yield to God and allow Him to fashion you as it pleases Him! It starts first with recognizing where you are in the process? You must take one of the following steps:

Get ON the wheel! This is for those who have been reluctant to get started.

Get BACK ON the wheel! Have you started and said this is hard and got off? Get back on and pray for the grace to endure.

STAY ON the wheel! You are in the middle of the process and God is working in you and fashioning you into the vessel that pleases Him.

Affirmation

"God mold me as it pleases You."

It Takes Work

> *Not as though I had already attained, either were already perfect: but I follow after, if that I may apprehend that for which also I am apprehended of Christ Jesus. Brethren, I count not myself to have apprehended: but this one thing I do, forgetting those things which are behind, and reaching forth unto those things which are before, I press toward the mark for the prize of the high calling of God in Christ Jesus.*
> **PHILIPPIANS 3:12-14 KJV**

Returning home from Jerusalem after the Feast of the Passover, Joseph and Mary discovered Jesus was missing. They returned to Jerusalem and after three days of frantically searching, they found him in the temple, sitting amid the teachers. Imagine the panic of a parent not being able to locate their child. "Son, why have you done this to us?" Having had my son wander off in a crowd before, I can relate to Mary's concern. 12-year-old Jesus said to them, "why did you seek me? Did you know that I must be about My Father's business?" They were left amazed because they did not understand what He spoke to them.

It was not His appointed time yet, but Jesus knew and was committed to completing the assignment He had been called to. Jesus was passionate as He expressed in John 9:4 "I must work the works of Him that sent me, while it is day: the night cometh, when no man can work." Jesus knew what we must also come into agreement with: God's plans for our lives will not just happen! You and I play a vital part in working on the works He has called us to.

Throughout scripture, there are references to work and how faith without works is dead. In Colossians 3:23, we are challenged to work heartily as unto the Lord and not men.

In Ecclesiastes, we are challenged by Solomon to do whatever we put our hands to with all our might. In Luke 10:7, we are reminded that a laborer is worthy of his hire. We do not work to earn our salvation; our work is evidence of our faith in Christ. In Philippians 3:12-14, Paul describes his work to become like Christ.

Forget those things that are behind.

While it is a great thing to look back over our lives to remember and reflect on God's goodness towards us, it is not healthy when looking back causes us to become stagnant. We must continue to press on.

Reach for things that are before.

If we are still breathing, God is not done with us. The unlimited possibilities to be used by God. Run hard after the work God has given you to do.

Press toward the mark.

The promises of God are ours, and His plans are ours, but does that mean the world will step aside and let us have them. There will be opposition. So it will take perseverance, but God empowers us to fight the good fight of faith.

One of my greatest challenges in obtaining the promises was having my mind renewed. After years of negative thinking, my mind wanted to go back to what was its norm but I became determined to daily encourage myself. God promised me hope and a future and it was mine! It will not be by power, nor by might, but by the power of the Holy Spirit, you will please the Father and receive your rewards.

Affirmation

"God is at work in me to fulfill His good purpose."

Redeem The Time

> *See then that you walk circumspectly, not as fools, but as wise, redeeming the time, because the days are evil.*
> *EPHESIANS 5:15-16 KJV*

During a bible study, the teacher made a significant distinction between a robber and a thief. Although both involve taking someone else's property, he explained how the robber uses violence, force, or threat to steal and the thief is often unsuspecting when it steals from others. You will not mistake if you are being robbed because of its violent nature, but a thief will blindside you, leaving you speechless.

Procrastinating is an act or habit of putting off or delaying doing what you should. It is an intentional act. Song of Solomon 2:15 warns us to be aware of the little foxes that spoil the vine and cause a substantial loss. Procrastination is one of life's little foxes. Time is a nonrenewable resource! We must redeem the time. If and when God impresses upon you to do something, obey. Timing is key with God and when you procrastinate you are operating in disobedience. Yes, delayed obedience is still disobedience!

I grew up with major trust issues because I was unable to trust those I should have been able to depend on to protect, provide, and nurture me. When I began my relationship with God, those trust issues did not magically disappear. I was afraid to fully trust God. I feared He would be like the others I had trusted. I feared displeasing Him because I could not handle the rejection. When opportunities presented themselves to move out in faith, I did nothing and chose to play it safe. I began to do "good things" but not the "God thing" I was being challenged to pursue.

Being so afraid to displease or to miss God caused me to sit dormant for years with books and ministries in me. I was full of gifts, passions, and good intentions but paralyzed by fear and insecurities. I was operating in disobedience and not because I did not love God but because I was overcome by negative emotions and self-talk.

Numerous times I have had to sit back and watch someone enjoy the spoils from an idea I was given but buried. The rewards could have been mine had I responded immediately. It forced me to get before God and deal with the thief that was robbing me of my blessings. Procrastination was doing more harm than good. I, Adecia, was the weapon formed against me, causing me not to prosper. It is time to have a sense of urgency about matters before you. If you are not experiencing the fullness of God, seek Him on what it is that's taking from you.

I have missed opportunities because of fear and fear of being rejected. I now pray, "God, I want your will." Simple. Then I proceeded to do what was impressed upon me. You may recall the phrase "do it afraid" I say "do it in faith!" Be bold to step out in faith on some issues, not knowing what the end will be simply because it is better than not doing anything at all. Your obedience to God makes whatever you are doing a success.

Here is some good news: Proverbs 6:31 says when a thief is found, he must restore sevenfold; he must give up all the wealth of his house. Identify what has been robbing you and demand to be repaid!

Affirmation

"I am a good steward of my time."

I Am Not An Island

> *For in fact the body is not one member but many.*
> *1 CORINTHIANS 12:14 NKJV*

God puts people in our lives for a reason. In 2017 my Mother underwent a bone marrow transplant. We are originally from Louisiana, but after she retired from the U.S. Army, she decided to settle in Alabama near one of her prior duty stations. Her brother, who also is a U.S. Army retiree, was the only family we had in the state. From her diagnosis to the transplant and then on through her recovery, the undeniable message was: YOU NEED PEOPLE!

To say it was an overwhelming experience is an understatement. There was no way I would have been able to do it all alone.

It had only been a few months since she received her cancer diagnosis and as a family, we were still mentally processing that, and now we were preparing for this crucial procedure. Again, God puts people in our lives for a reason!

My mother required a special diet and for the first 30 days home she had to be quarantined. I was still working full-time and needed and welcomed the help. Her longtime friend immediately stepped up to be the one who would take her to all her appointments. Our church family and her friends purchased and cooked meals which freed me to focus more on her care. Friends came over and cleaned her house and car.

There were countless prayers, hospital visitations, and errand runners. My ex-husband and his wife kept our children for the two weeks leading up to the transplant allowing me to prepare the home for my mother's return. Once home, family members came and became vital caregivers. 12

There was no stone unturned concerning my mother's needs. Looking back, I appreciated the help, but it was not easy to receive it. I had been too prideful before to ask or even accept help when I knew I needed it, but my mother's experience opened my eyes to the fact that I was not an island and how much I needed others. I had to resolve that it was okay to receive help.

My cousin and I did a series on Facebook live on "The Power of Two," stressing the importance of relationships. We reflected on the book of Mark, and when Jesus sent the disciples out, He sent them two by two. As the Body of Christ, we are all members of one body. Throughout scripture, we are encouraged to have love one for another. The eye needs the hand, the head needs the feet, and if one suffers, every other part suffers along with it. Working along with others is commanded; having the right people in your life is a blessing.

The growth in letting others in has been phenomenal. Yes, I use wisdom and always seek God when I let others in because I want those around me who have pure motives. But my family's experience made me more sensitive to the needs of others.

I am a giver and I love to be a blessing to others. I let my walls down and invited in those God had sent to be a blessing to me. Some of the best gifts God gives us are the people he sends. I call them my Divine Connections. Pray God will send individuals in your life where each of you will enhance what God is doing in the other.

Affirmation

"God is sending the right people into my life."

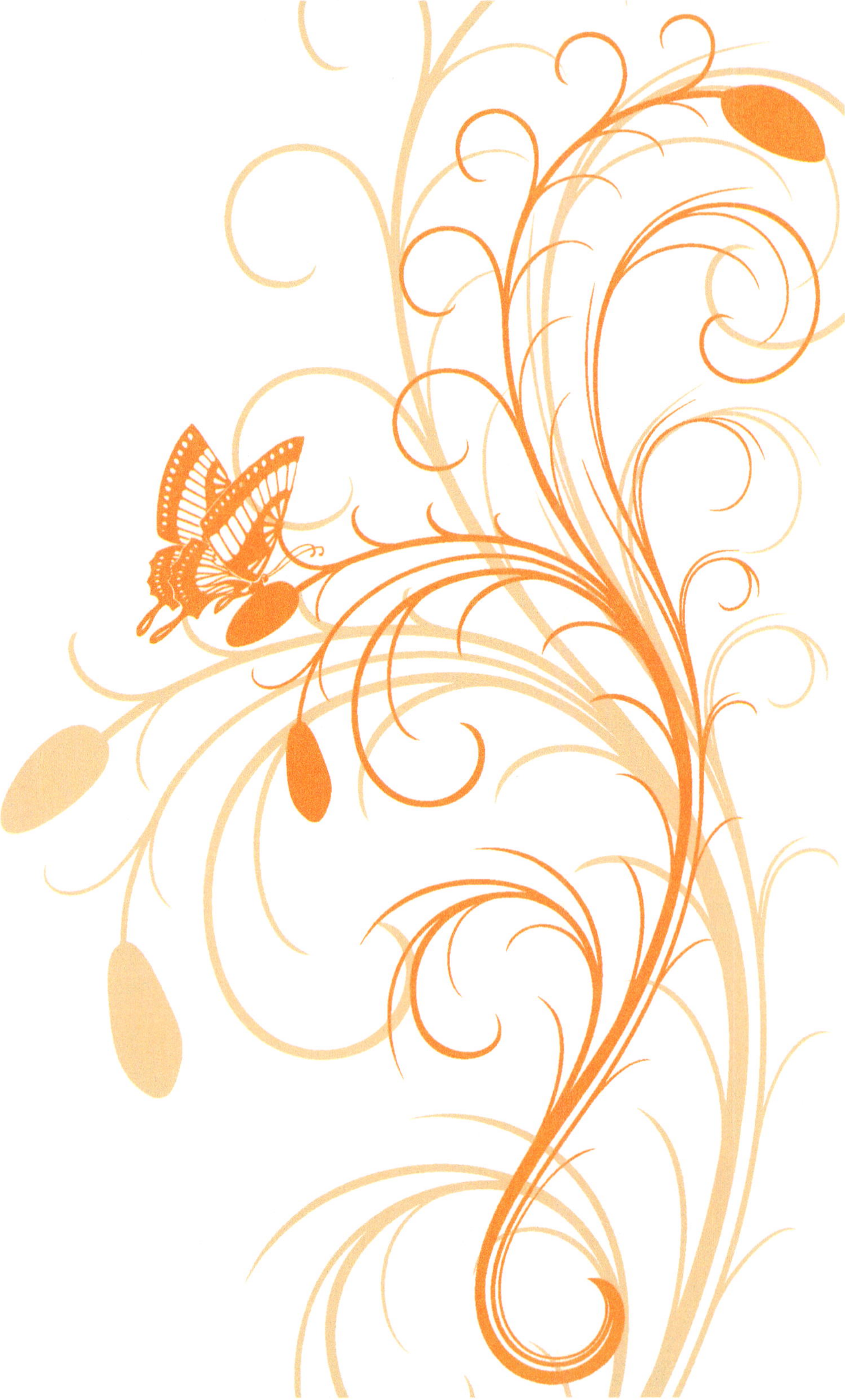

Embrace Differences

> *After these things I looked, and behold, a great multitude which no one could number, of all nations, tribes, peoples, and tongues, standing before the throne and before the Lamb, clothed with white robes, with palm branches in their hands.* REVELATIONS 7:9 NKJV

John 3:16, one of the most well-known and memorized verses in the bible, gives us a depiction of the heart of God. It is written, "For God so loved the world that he gave His only begotten Son, that whosoever believeth in Him should not perish, but have everlasting life." You read correctly. It said God so loved THE WORLD. The Apostle John, in the book of Revelation, gives a vision of that promise fulfilled when he describes the multitude standing before the throne. There were representatives from every nation, tribe, people group, and language—all important to God, there to witness the Lamb of God.

My twins' 8th-grade field trip was to the Tennessee Aquarium in Chattanooga. There are over 33,000 fish species alone worldwide and I believe Chattanooga had a sample of each of them there that day. I was more captivated than my children as I beheld the different species, colors, and sizes, each with intricate details distinguishing them from others. That was just the fish.

The species of birds were just as amazing! Truthfully, if it was me, we probably would have had maybe seven species with about different 20 different colors of each for some flair, but our God is one of a kind and His work is unmatched. He went into detail with each one making it unique and special. The beauty of creation indeed bears witness to the awesomeness of our God. I left the aquarium enlightened and with a newfound reverence for God and a deep admiration for the people, He professed were beautifully and wonderfully created as well.

As a military family, we traveled abroad and my brother and I encountered many people from different social, cultural, economic, and ethnic groups. We experienced the food, music, dance, clothing, and much more of many cultures up close and personal throughout our travels. I was reminded that the earth is the LORD's and the fullness thereof and all its people.

For the kingdom's sake, we do not ever want to box ourselves in and limit how God can use us to reach multitudes. We should desire to be a willing vessel, ready to pour into whomever God places on our path. I am unapologetic about who I am, who God has created me to be as we all should be equally proud as God's prized creation.

Differences are not to be afraid of but something that we should embrace if we are going to fulfill our mission to make disciples of all men. I am grateful to God and the marvelous works of His hands. Appreciating the beauty of God's work in another does not diminish His wonderful work in us.

God is love and He sent Jesus as a testament of His love. It is necessary that as we go out as Ambassadors of Christ, we realize the power of embracing those we are called to and seeing each individual as God sees them.

Affirmation

"I love because God first loved me."

Handfuls On Purpose

> *And let fall also some of the handfuls of purpose for her, and leave them, that she may glean them, and rebuke her not.* RUTH 2:16 KJV

In the Book of Ruth, we see how God the Father rewards faithfulness. Ruth had proved her love and faithfulness early on by leaving her pagan culture to follow her mother-in-law Naomi and Naomi's God, Yahweh, the God of Israel. Naomi had lost her husband and both sons, one of which was Ruth's husband, therefore as two widows, they were ripe for the blessings of God.

Returning to Bethlehem at the beginning of the barley harvest, Ruth requested to go and glean in the fields of Boaz. Boaz, a man of great wealth, was a kinsman, a blood relative of Naomi's husband. Ruth was intentional in choosing Boaz's field "please let me go to the field, and glean head of grain after him in whose sight I may find favor." And she found favor with Boaz! Boaz saw how she diligently worked and inquired of her. He also protected her from the young men, ordered them to give her water to drink, and invited her in at mealtime. He acknowledged her sacrifice to leave her culture, people, and language because of her love for Naomi. He blessed her, declaring that because she sought refuge from the God of Israel, the LORD would repay her with a full reward.

God used Boaz to redeem Ruth. Because of her faithfulness, she gained a husband and son. Her son, Obed, was the grandfather of King David. In the book of Matthew, Ruth is listed along in the genealogy of Jesus. Naomi nor Ruth knew the plans God had when they returned to Israel, but God had gone before them and made provision.

Ruth is an inspiration to do good for goodness sake. God is not an unjust God. He will not forget your labor of love and how you have helped His people and continue to show His people love. He will honor your efforts, so become OK with being abundantly blessed. Boaz ordered the men to let bundles of grain fall on purpose for Ruth. She was purposely given more than enough to take home for herself and Naomi.

When you see the hand of God actively work in your life, praise Him. He will indeed pour out blessings you will not have room enough to receive. Our God is not average. He is a God of abundance who has richly blessed us with spiritual and natural blessings. Expect God to be good to you. In Psalm 67, the psalmist makes a plea for God's blessings "God be merciful to us and bless us, and cause His face to shine upon us."

What Ruth did for Naomi was done in secret and out of love. She did not honor her for a reward but God rewarded Ruth openly. He sees the things you do in secret. He is aware and has recorded your faithfulness. In His grace, God gives us what we do not deserve because it is who He is. Increase your capacity to receive and expect handfuls on purpose. You have been chosen because of His faithfulness.

Can you stand to be blessed!

Affirmation

"God shines His light on me."

Overcome

> *As it is written, for thy sake we are killed all the day long; we are accounted as sheep for the slaughter. Nay, in all these things we are more than conquerors through him that loved us.* ROMANS 8:36–37 KJV

Being a believer in Christ does not exempt one from life's difficulties. In Romans Chapter 8, Paul reminds the believers there would be troubles, sufferings, persecutions, famines, lack, dangers, and more along their Christian walk. Yet in all those things, they were more than conquerors through Christ.

Overcoming is the expectation for believers because of the greater one who lives in and is at work in us. When I ran high school track, there was a point in the race when the weight of the contest got the best of us, and after the race, our coach would say, "the monkey got on your back." We started great with flawless running form but somewhere coming up on the final stretches, it felt as if something had hopped on our backs for the ride. Thirty years later, I laugh even now because it was a real thing. We could almost time when the pressure would hit our teammates during the race.

You too are in a race and at some point, you will have to get the monkey off your back and finish strong. The issues of life will want to hop on for the ride, but we have to fight on to finish our race. I recall a sermon I heard, "Grow From What You Go Through," which challenged the listeners to take lessons from what they had gone through and MOVE ON!

Whether the challenges you face are spiritually, financially, physically, or emotionally, Apostle Paul declares that greater is ahead. The word declares you are more than conquerors.

We have an unmatched support system in God, Jesus, and the Holy Spirit. We also have help among the body of believers who are also in the race. When we think we are the only ones going through something, it makes what we are going through seem unconquerable. Hence why the bible says we overcome by the word of our testimony. When we share how we have overcome, others are inspired. As we mature in our relationship with Christ, we will realize that things do not have the same effect on us that they did years, months, or even days ago. We must trust God and receive His help in all things. As a former American History teacher, I can assure you that losing a battle does not mean you have lost the war. As a nation, we lost many but ultimately won the war.

We will win by our unwavering faith in the promises of God to work all things out for our good. We fight by knowing the Word. When we commit to prayer, it is in His presence that we will receive our battle strategy. As you continue your race, use the battles you have won as your motivation to continue running!

In the war for our eternal souls, Jesus has already secured that victory. The war has been won. But while we are here on earth, we will have some battles as we fulfill God's purpose for our lives. Like Paul's thorns, we will have challenges along our walk, the Bible speaks of this, but God promised to never leave nor forsake us while we are going through. Cast any behaviors, attitudes, mindsets, beliefs, tendencies, etc., which are not beneficial to sustaining your victory at the feet of Jesus. There is a lot more to accomplish and a lot more to overcome.

Affirmation

"I am an overcomer."

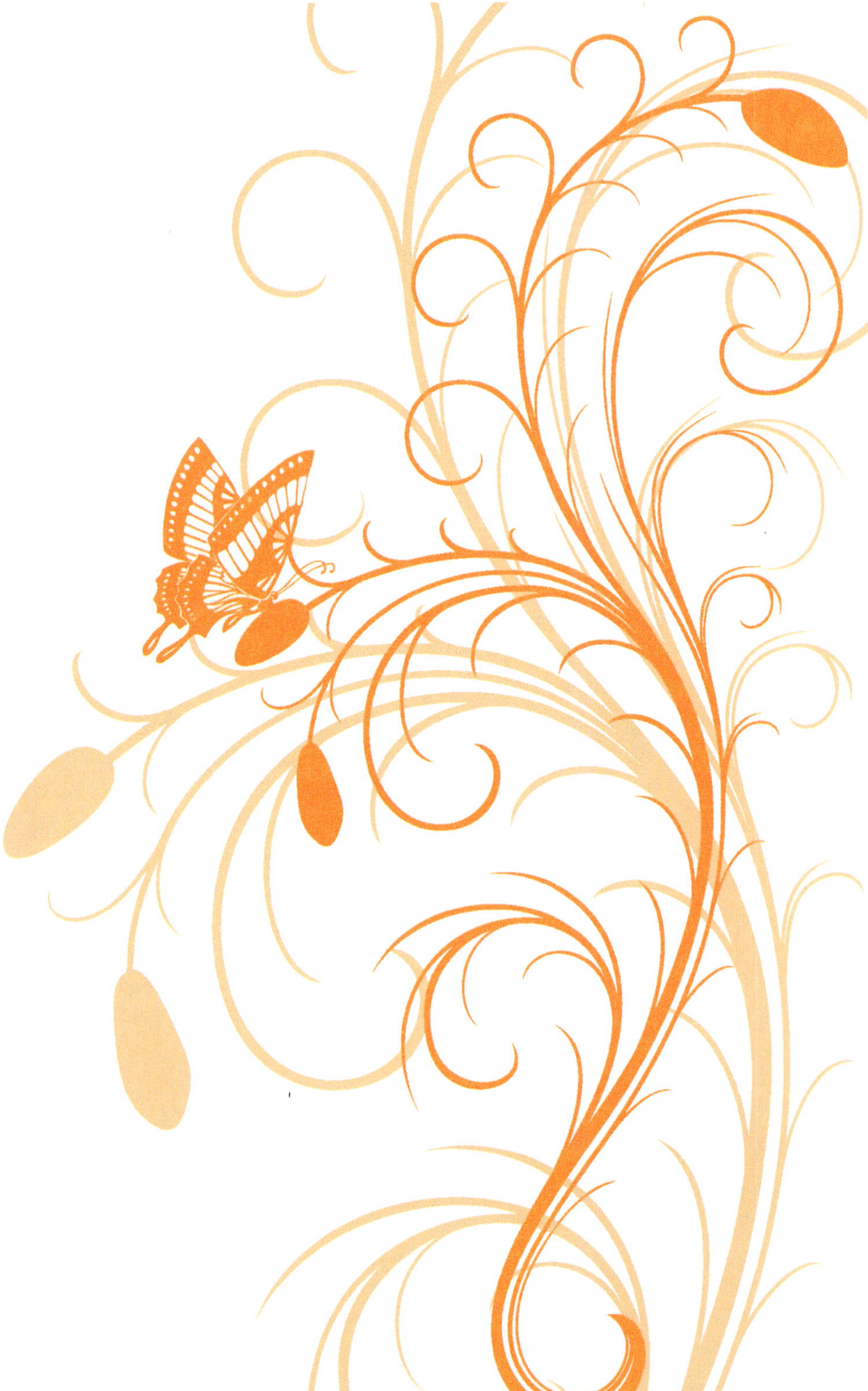

Perfected Peace

> *You will keep him in perfect peace, whose mind is stayed on You, because he trusts in You.* ISAIAH 26:3 NKJV

Everything around us is subject to change with little to no warning. Our finances, jobs and businesses, relationships, and leisure activities are all one crisis from everything falling apart or having to be realigned. The global pandemic proved this to be true as millions experienced losses, in many areas, with many a few years later still trying to make sense of it all and regain stability.

In Isaiah 26, the song celebrates the defeat of Judah's enemy, and verse 3 expresses a promise that is echoed throughout scripture: if we trust God and keep our minds stayed on Him that we not only have peace, but God would keep us in perfect peace. A powerful testament of God's trustworthiness to keep us and to give us peace amid storms. Peace is a state of existence. To take a position of peace, we have an inner witness that is unmoved by circumstances. We take our rest in God and can declare, "it is well with my soul."

I never imagined I would have to live during a pandemic. I had read about them in my history classes and read of those during biblical times, but at no point did I see it as a reality for me. Naturally, I was concerned about how to govern myself and my children.

At the beginning of the pandemic, when many churches were closing, our ministry never stopped our Saturday morning corporate prayer. The word tells us men should always pray and this was not the time we would stop.

Those of us who met there regularly sought God on behalf of the body of Christ and the nations because we knew God was not caught off guard by what the world was experiencing and if we were going to fight this invisible enemy we would need His wisdom. During a time of global uncertainty, panic, and weariness, we found our peace in Him.

If fear of the unknown is not countered with the truth of God's trustworthiness, you will deprive yourselves of peace. But the peace of God, if embraced, will guard your heart and mind. Jesus, the Prince of Peace, offers us indescribable peace. Jesus kept His calm in the most trying situations. He never flew into a rage. There is also no mention of Him worrying or being stressed out over anything! When they sought to kill Him and when Jesus was constantly challenged and questioned by the religious leaders, He answered them but maintained His peace. Jesus's response was to steal away and commune with God. Prayer was His lifestyle and how He managed the daily demands of the people. And let us not forget how He slept during a turbulent storm. That same peace is our portion, and Jesus, our example, shows us that we can live in that peace in the most trying of times.

It matters where you go or who you look to in times of uncertainty. Everything around you will not always be ideal, but you must pursue peace within yourself as you pursue peace with others. Perfect peace belongs to those who trust God and find shelter in Him during troubles.

Affirmation

"God you are my peace. I trust You."

Live In The Moment

> *Come now, you who say, "Today or tomorrow we will go to such and such a city, spend a year there, buy and sell, and make a profit"; whereas you do not know what will happen tomorrow. For what is your life? It is even a vapor that appears for a little time and then vanishes away. Instead, you ought to say, "If the Lord wills, we shall live to do this or that."* **JAMES 4:13–15 NKJV**

My coworker had visited a museum while vacationing with his family and told of this one family's teenage son was on the phone for the entirety of the tour and missed all of the historical artifacts. What is a once-in-a-lifetime trip for some was of no interest to him. Instead of enjoying the experience with his family, whatever was on his phone had his undivided attention. I was not too critical of the teenager. I too have missed many opportunities because my mind was in many places and not in the moment. With all the constant distractions around us because of the 24-hour access to "breaking news" right at our fingertips. The constant distractions present challenges to focus; to be successful in this season demands discipline.

It was my son's birthday and I remember being frustrated because he would not remain still so I could capture the perfect picture to post to social media. When I would position one child another would move and this went on for a while until I had to say forget it and settled for what I had. I had spent time and money to make the day a memorable one for us all and here I was ruining the moment because I had to get the money shot. I was immediately convicted and promised to never miss a present moment with my children.

We have created many memories after that day some I have pictures of and others I have captured in my heart. James 4:13-15 warns the readers not to boast about tomorrow. "Today I'm going to this; tomorrow I'm going to do that" when we have no idea what will happen tomorrow. Because God is the author of our tomorrow, it should be said, "If the Lord wills."

James is not telling the readers not to plan for the future but rather to enjoy where they are right now! In the book of Matthew, Jesus teaches not to take no thought for tomorrow because tomorrow has enough trouble of its own. Simply put, trust God. Have a new level of gratefulness and appreciation for Him. If the focus is on what I want to have or where I want to be, we will miss out on where God is currently at work in our lives.

As believers, we need to take in and enjoy the moments and people God provides. When Jesus taught the disciples how to pray, he told them to pray, give me this day my daily bread. The model prayer instructed them to pray and to trust God to provide for their daily natural and spiritual needs.

Again, am I saying do not consider tomorrow or do not plan for tomorrow: NO! I am saying do not stress over tomorrow. I have been so concerned over if I would have enough for tomorrow that I did not thank God for the provision I already had for the day. In Exodus 16, God told Moses he would rain bread from heaven and he would send meat for the people and they were to gather what they needed for that day. They were not to take any of it to keep for tomorrow for God would provide. They were coming out of Egypt and he wanted them to trust Him to take care of them. Despite Moses's plea to them to not hide any of it because the Lord would provide more the next day, some did it anyway.

The Lord had provided their daily bread and given them more than enough for that day, but their minds were on their tomorrow. Instead of relishing in the miracle of what God had done, they were concerned if He would be able to do it again. Do not be robbed of today worrying about tomorrow. Our God is faithful and He will provide. Enjoy every day and in it give thanks. Do not take life, people, and moments for granted.

Affirmation

"Lord, I am grateful and I praise You for this day."

Rest

And on the seventh day God ended His work which He had done, and He rested on the seventh day from all His work which He had done. GENESIS 2:2 NKJV

Rest is defined as ceasing from work or movement to relax, refresh oneself, or recover strength. In Genesis Chapter 2, on the seventh day, God rested. Everything He needed to create was in place. He saw and beheld it was good, so He ceased from His work. That day of rest or Sabbath day, God deemed holy and He ordained rest for His people to cease their works. Jesus rested. He went about the lands healing, saving, and delivering people from all manners of sicknesses and diseases and He often broke away from the crowd to a solitary place in God's presence to replenish.

Jesus also called His disciples to rest after they had returned from ministering. God ordained rest for the land. The people could sow and gather for six years, but on the seventh year, the land was to have a year of rest. If God cared enough about the health of the land, how much more does He care about our wellbeing.

God did not rest because He was tired but because His work was finished. We are human and become tired; our physical bodies require rest. Our bodies must rest for a period where we cease from the busyness and demands of the day and recover. When we sleep our body begins to repair itself. Cells are refreshed and restored, our brains can now store new information and rid themselves of toxic waste.

There's a series of necessary changes that must occur, which is vital to our overall health. When our bodies are lacking rest and rejuvenation, it causes problems. Our responses are delayed, we may not think as clearly, and we may see a breakdown in our immune systems, leading to illnesses. We are warned not to operate heavy machinery without proper rest because of the danger it may cause if we are not fully alert.

Spiritual rest is just as vital to our overall wellbeing. It is a time of spiritual refreshing and resetting that also helps us to function properly. It is in God that we live, move, and have our being. We are not sustaining ourselves. It is the power of God that quickens our mortal bodies keeping us from exhaustion. We must rest in Him. It is an intentional act whereby we see God as the source of strength, and as Jesus modeled, we pull away to stay connected to our life-giving Father.

I am a mother, professional, ministry leader, entrepreneur, and author, and all those roles have daily demands. I have ended days overworked, stressed, and drained from trying to make it all happen. I have gone overboard trying to change people, myself, and circumstances in my strength when the Bible clearly states it will not be by power or might but by the spirit of the Lord. So physically, spiritually, and mentally, I had to cease my works and find rest in Him.

I am currently in a season of rest where I have been called to limit my activities and God has called me closer to know Him more. I have been called to get more into His word. The call to come closer has pulled me out of the rat race of life and has been a much-needed time of refocusing and awareness of what matters the most and what I should be giving my time and efforts.

Time is too valuable to labor in vain. God is calling us back into alignment with Him and His purpose for our lives. I was out of position, doing things because they were good things, but they were not what God had assigned for the season I was in. After repenting and getting back in the will of God, there was a rest that came upon my soul. Knowing Him is more important than what we can do for Him. Matter-of-factly, the greater we know, the more He will enhance our works.

Affirmation

"I rest in God."

Blessed To Be A Blessing

> *God be merciful to us and bless us, and cause His face to shine upon us. Selah* PSALM 67:1 NKJV

I have always seen myself as a servant and have operated with the mindset that my life is not my own. I am currently a ministry leader, but I was a middle school classroom teacher before assuming my role within the church. I later received a graduate degree in Clinical Psychology, so my educational background has always been intent on helping others. One of the characteristics I used to describe myself is "facilitator," because I am, without question, a helper. The psalmist in Psalm 67:1 asks God for His mercy and blessings.

It was not a selfish request. By way of the blessings and favor of God upon his life, it would provoke others to praise God.

God uses us people to help people. Partnering with God is the best team we can form. I have been on quite a few teams as a high school and collegiate athlete, but they do not measure up to the victories God and I have won. I thank God that he sees us as worthy partners and blesses us to do good works. We are abundantly blessed!

Why does God bless us? So we may praise Him. When we share the good news and use what we have been given to be a blessing to others, we are giving God praise. The natural and spiritual blessings of God are to glorify Him. When God blesses us, it is to impact those He has assigned to us. God gave us Jesus. Jesus gave up His life. We should be willing to give of ourselves with a sincere desire to pour into the lives of others. There are many ways we can bless others! The simplest things from a smile, hello, text, or kind words can inspire a heart.

Ways we can praise God:

Time: Make serving God a priority. My Saturday mornings are booked for corporate prayer unless I am out of town for work or family. I have three teenagers, so I do not have as much free time as I did as a single and unmarried believer, but I use my available time to serve as I am needed. Once you make your relationship with God and His people a priority, you will find the time to serve.

Talents: There is always ministry work to be done! The needs of the body and community are oftentimes more than those who are willing to help. No one should feel slighted as if their gifts, talents, and abilities are not needed. God would not have blessed you as He has and placed you where you are if there was not a need for what you possess. The opportunities to serve in the kingdom are plentiful. It is only the laborers who are few.

Treasures: Financially support the working of the ministry with your tithes and offerings. Finances are needed to assist in advancing the Kingdom of God. I have always told others I would sow millions into the kingdom and I believe I will. Now the particulars on how God is going to create the opportunity for me to do so have not been revealed yet, but I am convinced it will. It only takes one God-inspired seed for it to manifest. Freely we have received, freely we should give.

Affirmation

"I am blessed to be a blessing."

Victory In Obedience

> *Also I heard the voice of the Lord, saying, Whom shall I send, and who will go for us? Then said I, here am I; send me. ISAIAH 6:8 KJV*

You valuable are to God, He has use for you. How should you respond to God's call? The prophet Isaiah responded in humble adoration, "here am I; send me." Likewise, we should respond accordingly, "here I am." Isaiah had just experienced a personal encounter with God. He saw the Lord, high and exalted on a throne with the train of His robe filling the temple. In the light of God's glory, Isaiah had a clear view of his uncleanness. His repentant cry led to his deliverance. When the seraphim touched his mouth with a live coal, his guilt was taken away and his sins were atoned for. Then he heard the Lord saying, "Whom shall I send and who will go for us," Isaiah eagerly responded, here am I, send me and he was commissioned.

There is work to be done and God is looking for willing vessels. Whatever God has called you to do, you have already been equipped to do it. Isaiah was immediately commissioned once he accepted the call. He had no time to second guess or disqualify himself, God knew what He would do in and through Isaiah because of his obedience.

I am reminded of the television character MacGyver and his Tinker Swiss army knife. MacGyver was a genius! There was not a problem he could not solve or an enemy he could not defeat. The awesomeness was not in MacGyver but in the weapons he chose to defeat his enemies and get out of tricky situations. He found a use for paper clips, gum, duct tape, birthday candles, matches, whatever was available.

For believers, God has also given us unusual weapons to wage war against our enemies. 2 Corinthians 10:4 "for the weapons of our warfare are not carnal, but mighty through God to the pulling down of strongholds." God will give us the battle strategy. Our only job is to listen and respond in obedience.

There was no battle at the battle of Jericho. God told Joshua he had already delivered Jericho into their hands before they stepped foot in the city, but they would be victorious if they fought God's way. The Israelites were to march around the city walls once a day for six days and on the seventh day, seven times and at Joshua's command, the people were to shout. The people were obedient to what God instructed and He gave them victory. The people of Judah did not have to fight. God instructed them to praise. The people sang and praised God and their enemies began to take each other out.

There are countless testimonies of victories over physical and spiritual enemies when we trust in God's power to be our defense. Go to God and get the battle strategy for whatever is challenging you. His answer may be prayer, praise, worship, fasting, or another weapon. Whatever strategy He gives to you, obey! Even if it does not make sense to you, your obedience to Him will assure you victory. Trust God when you have to go into battle. He will give you what to do or say and He will also fight along with you.

Affirmation

"Thanks be to God who gives me the victory."

Ask Big

> *Now this is the confidence that we have in Him, that if we ask anything according to His will, He hears us. And if we know that He hears us, whatever we ask, we know that we have the petitions that we have asked of Him.*
> **1 JOHN 5:14-15 NKJV**

"God wants to bless me more than I want to be blessed." Sitting in a friend's church some years ago the guest speaker had the congregation make the declaration. I said it out of obedience to his command though I did not have the faith at the time to believe it. Still, I aspired to. Fast forward, I now know enough of God's word to know He does desire to bless me more than I think I deserve to be blessed. He proves it by daily loading me and you with benefits because He is just that kind of God. He is without a doubt able to do exceeding, abundantly above all we could even ask or think.

In Matthew 20:20-22 the mother of Zebedee's sons brought them to Jesus, knelt before Him, and asked a favor of Him. Jesus asked, "what is it you want" and without reservation, she asked Jesus to have her sons be a part of His kingdom but she did not stop there. She asked if her sons could sit one at Jesus's right hand and the other at His left. Bold request! Jesus replied, "You do not know what you are asking, can you drink the cup? the brothers replied, "we can." Jesus said they would indeed drink from His cup, but to sit at His right or left was not His to grant. It would be given to those whom the Father had prepared them." She asked BIG!

In a grocery store parking lot one day, I began singing, "Exceedingly. Abundantly. I take the limits off you, LORD. I take the limits off you, LORD. Exceedingly. Abundantly," and kept repeating it. I cannot recall where the inspiration came from. It was my song from the Lord that day and it became my prayer to Him, "Lord, help me to take the limits off of You. Increase my capacity for the exceeding, abundantly."

At the time, I was preparing to speak at a women's conference, and God impressed upon me that He desired to do more than we were expecting. I thought we had high expectations, but God wanted us to truly have a glory-to-glory moment and live up to the conference's name. I have been called overzealous but I just believe in God so I was ready for whoever He chose to move!

I refuse to put limits on what God can do in and through us. Jesus had all power, but the scriptures tell us He did not work many miracles in Nazareth because of the people's unbelief! It was not because of a lack of power or His will to do so but because the people lacked faith.

Personally, professionally, ministerially, and financially, I desire God's absolute best. I want what He wants for me. I am convinced my dreams for my life do not compare to what He has willed for me. Begin praying for God's will for your life. Take the limits off because He is able! Little children have the grandest imagination. They believe and dream big. Go before your Father with childlike faith. Make your requests known!

Affirmation

"LORD, bless me as only You can."

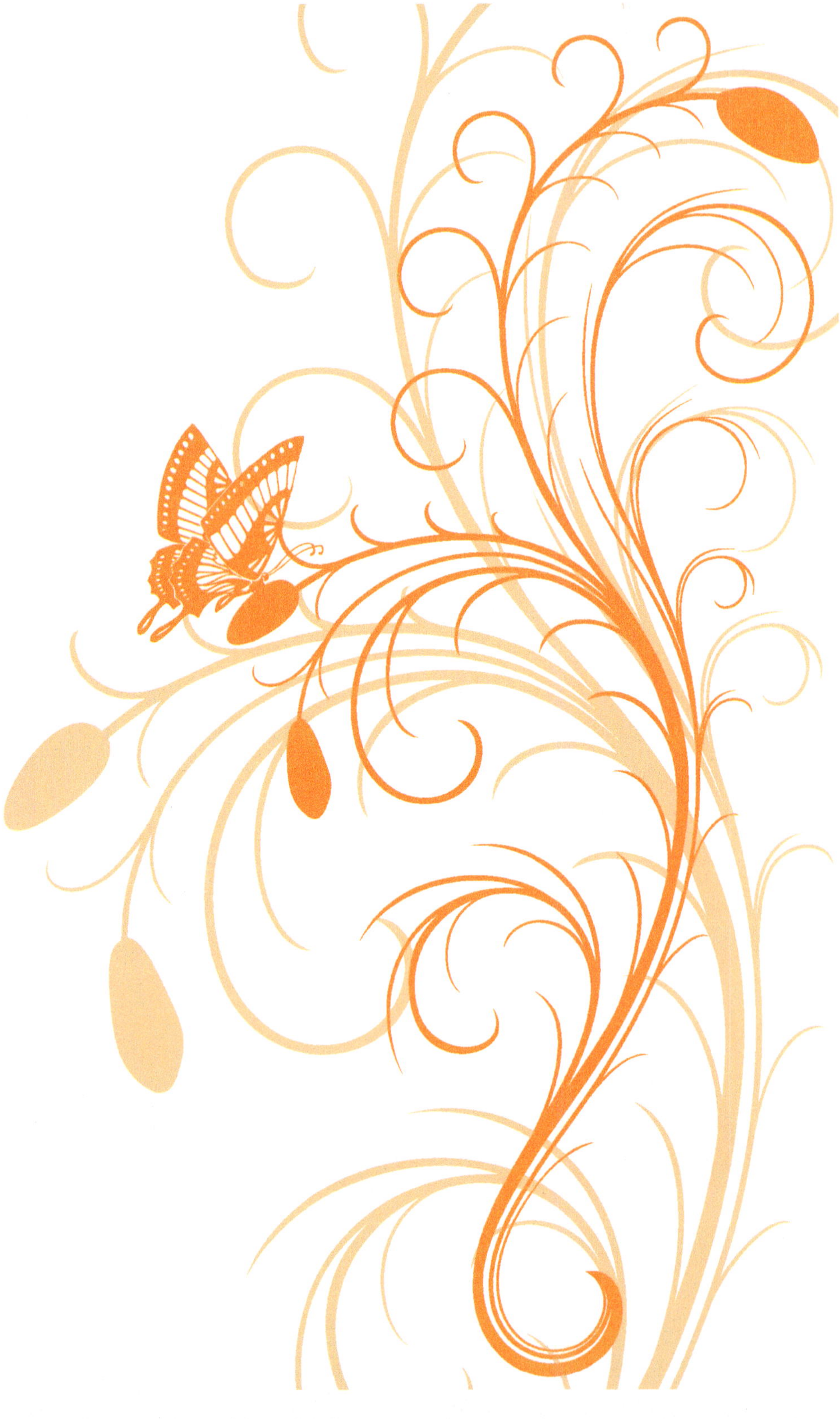

Forgive Early And Often

> *And be kind to one another, tenderhearted, forgiving one another, even as God in Christ forgave you.*
> **EPHESIANS 4:32 NKJV**

God showed His great love for us by sending Christ to die for us. While we were yet sinners, He forgave us. Before we were aware of our sin and asked for forgiveness, it was already done through Jesus's death at Calvary. The foundation of our faith is built on the power of forgiveness.

It is impossible to move through life and not experience some form of pain. Whether intentional or unintentional, no one is exempt from hurt. In establishing personal, business, and professional relationships, there will be opportunities to offend and be offended, but there should always be efforts made to resolve any issues.

When you decide to live on purpose and experience the fullness of life, you have to watch for dream killers. Unforgiveness is a dream killer and can kill success. The key to not allowing unforgiveness to have dominion in your life is to forgive early and often. Forgiveness is tough and even more challenging when you have justifiable reasons to not forgive, but unforgiveness is too costly. Unforgiveness will have you rehearsing and stuck in the past when the blessings of God are ahead of you.

Forgive Early. If you do not deal with the offense early on, you will nurse it and it can become dangerous. In some medical books, unforgiveness is treated as a disease because it makes people sick! It can decrease blood flow to the heart. If left unchallenged, the anger, bitterness, or even depression from it can break down the immune system. At the onset of the hurt, deal with it then or as soon as you recognize it. Forgive early to not allow bitterness to take root in your heart. You do not have to pretend you were not hurt but do not allow it to continue to rob you of your joy.

Forgive Often. In the book of Matthew, Peter came up to Jesus and asked him, "Lord, how shall my brother sin against me, and I forgive him? As many as seven times?" I wonder if Peter thought he was impressing Jesus by saying he would forgive seven times. Jesus answered him, "not seven, I tell you, but seventy times seven." Did Jesus mean that after forgiving someone 490 times that one would then be able to not forgive? It is not what He meant at all, but the Kingdom of God deals with the attitude of the heart. God is a merciful God and has forgiven us. He commands us to behave likewise with one another. One of the last words of Christ from the cross was asking for forgiveness of those who caused Him horrifying sufferings.

Forgiveness should be pursued for your good. Christ came to set us free and unforgiveness is an unnecessary weight to carry around. When you purpose to forgive, it will be evident in your actions and attitudes. When I am upset, I have to remind myself, "Is what the person said or did worth forfeiting the promises of God?" No! You will have to put it into proper perspective because you have far too much to lose. No one is worth you missing out on all God has for you because you have chosen not to forgive.

God said cast all our cares on Him. He is a loving Father who knows and understands all that you have suffered. You cannot change what has happened to you, but you do have power over its continual impact on your life. Forgiveness may not result in a restored relationship and that is great in some circumstances. You should establish healthy boundaries!

Learn to forgive whether you feel the person has earned or deserved it. Choose to live in forgiveness because you only have control over what you do or say. Relieve yourself of any burdens of unforgiveness. Release it and walk in your freedom.

Affirmation

"I am forgiven therefore I choose to forgive."

Words Matter

Death and life are in the power of the tongue: and they that love it shall eat the fruit thereof. Proverbs 18:21 KJV

What are you telling yourself because your words matter! As a child, I remember a popular chant, "sticks and stones may break my bones, but words will never hurt me." The saying meant I will ignore you because you cannot hurt me with the unpleasant things you say. I did not understand then that physical pain will eventually subside, but words can stay with you for a lifetime. I no longer feel the pain of the childhood scar on my knee, but I can recall the hurtful words I heard over 40 years ago. It does not have the same effect it did as a child, but words do hurt. You have to be mindful of the words you speak to others and, more importantly, the words you speak over yourself.

Words are powerful. What we say sets the course of our lives. The goal is for the words you release to ripen, not rot. Proverbs 18:21 tells us we will eat the fruit of what we declare because there is power in what we speak. You must guard your words and speak those which will build up and not tear down. In Genesis, the earth was dark with no life or activity and God SPOKE. The marvelous creations we see on the earth were voice-activated. God said, and it was. You are commanded to speak the promises of God.

I love praying with my children and seeing how they light up when I begin to declare who they are according to the Word of God. I also encourage them to speak positively about themselves. I encourage them to consistently remind themselves that they are loved, beautiful, kind, intelligent, and favored by God. I do this because I know others will speak to them, and it will not always be kind, so empower them with what God has spoken because His words carry more weight

I have not always spoken positively about myself. It was a challenge because, for years, I continuously rehearsed the negative words of others. Their voice was louder than my own, louder than God's. I allowed their words to silence my own. Much of what was said was lies, but I did not refute any of it.

After dwelling on those words, it affected my behavior. I had become engulfed with what I was not. I had not given myself credit for the work I was doing to get to where I needed to be. But as I drew closer to God and allowed Him to redefine me, I learned how to separate what I did from who I was. I intentionally chose His truth over what they said.

The power is within you. Stir up, inspire, motivate, support, and give hope to YOU by the words you speak. The word of God is spirit and life. Find a promise which speaks to something you need to do. Come into agreement with what God said and begin to declare it. But do not just say it. Believe that God is a promise keeper, and He honors His word. Do not wait on anyone else. Permit yourself to be great. Speak life over everything you have been given stewardship over. The power of life and death lies in your tongue. Begin where you are calling out those things that are not as though they were.

Affirmation

"I am who God says I am."

Using My Gifts

> *For the kingdom of heaven is as a man travelling into a far country, who called his own servants, and delivered unto them his goods. And unto one he gave five talents, to another two, and to another one; to every man according to his several ability; and straightway took his journey.*
> **MATTHEW 25:14–15 KJV**

Keeping a chart of our athletes' weekly performances served as a powerful tool in getting them to show up to compete every week. We recorded their split times and distances as a measuring tool for the girls to use as motivation in improving their performances throughout the track season. While we would have gladly celebrated first place in each event, the objective was to have each athlete reach for a personal best in her event. So instead of focusing on placing first, second, or third at every track meet to receive a medal, our girls were encouraged to go after their personal best each week. With the focus on improving their times, it made them winners regardless of their place in the official race because they had improved.

It takes very little effort to unfairly compare ourselves to others, using their performance or progress as the measuring stick for where we should be in life or what we should have accomplished. The Master in Matthew Chapter 25 took into account each man's specific callings and abilities and gave them gifts accordingly. Each servant was trusted with the master's property and further in the story, the master came back expecting a return on the talent each received.

According to the Master, the servant with five talents and the servant with two talents were good and faithful servants because they had increased what they were given. Because of their faithfulness over the few, he made them a ruler over many.

The servants increased the master's investment. They demonstrated good stewardship over another man's goods. Regrettably, the servant with one talent expressed to the master that he was afraid to take a risk with his investment so he hid it. The master, disgusted, called the servant wicked and lazy because he did nothing with the talent he was given.

God has high expectations of the investments He has made in us. He is specific and intentional. He knows the purpose and plans He has for your life and He has gifted you accordingly. Now it is your responsibility to take what you have been given, be it five, two, or only one talent, and multiply the Master's investment! Your focus should be on identifying what you have been given and perfecting it to the full glory of God.

Like our track team's chart, daily assess if you are being the best you. Are you fully utilizing all that is within you? Have you made or are you working towards short and long-term goals to exhaust your talents? Do not be like the lazy and wicked servant who allowed fear to drive him to hide his talent. Do not be overly concerned with the affairs of others; the time is now to get busy investing in yourself!

Affirmation

"I am a good and faithful servant."

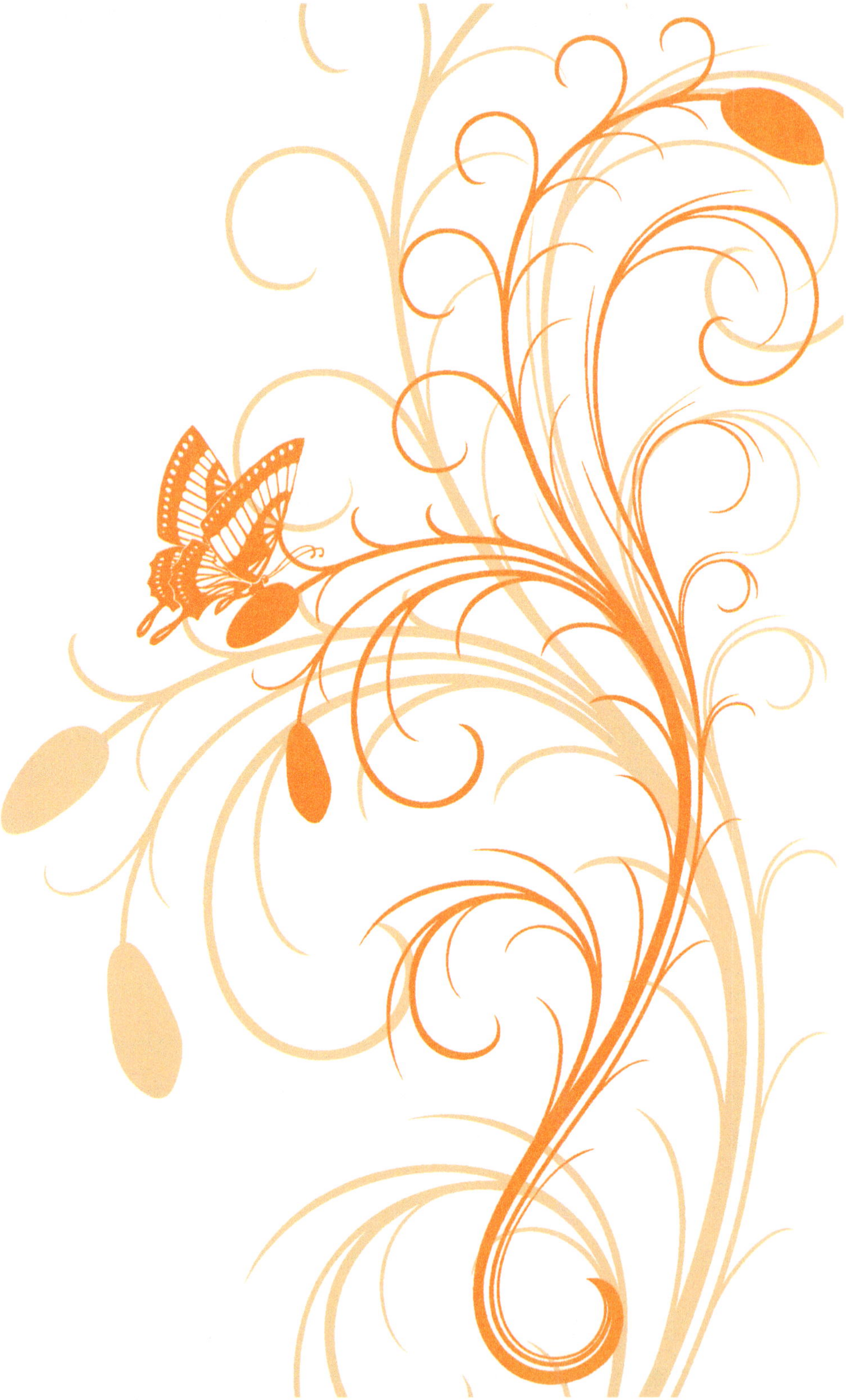

Willing To Be Misunderstood

> *For do I now persuade men, or God? or do I seek to please men? for if I yet pleased men, I should not be the servant of Christ.* GALATIANS 1:10 KJV

"I am not like that!" was my go-to response when hearing some untruth told about myself which was nowhere near the truth of who I was. I spent years bound by other people's opinions and countless efforts trying to get everyone to understand me. I tried to get to the root of every lie, often becoming frustrated from purely wanting to be understood. I eventually had to admit I was looking for acceptance!

Depending on your assignment and the sacrifices you may be called to make, it may not make sense to others. When you feel an urgency to separate from people, places, and things to draw closer to God, follow His leading even if it offends those closest to you. It is not personal and everyone will not understand. Therefore, what God is calling you to, should be of more importance than the need to be understood.

I have often heard, "it doesn't take all that," but I knew in my heart that for my assignment, it did! What those criticizing did not know was that I was not making all the sacrifices I should have been making. They questioned but I was determined to not let it hinder me from running after that which was mine. When you are intentional about your purpose, it will require a disciplined focus.

If anyone can relate to being misunderstood, it was Jesus, so you are in good company! In the gospel of Luke 4:18, when He declared the Spirit of the Lord was upon Him and began to tell of His purpose and what He was sent to do, many were confused.

The crowd who was once enamored with Him because He spoke so well, and was full of wisdom, now questioned, "Isn't this the son of Joseph." They had become familiar with Him because they knew His mother was Mary, and His father Joseph the carpenter, so how was it then that He was now the Son of God? How could He be King? But He was!

Jesus was unmoved by the opinion of the crowd. His response was, "no prophet is accepted in his hometown," and instead of staying there trying to make them believers, He went on and fulfilled His purpose. As with Paul in the book of Galatians, Jesus chose to please God and not men!

You have to follow Jesus and Paul's example by not allowing the misunderstanding of others to stop you from pursuing God. Unapologetically declare who you know you are in Him! Be intentional and purposeful about carrying out your assignment. Do not waste energy trying to make everyone ok with your decision to do what is best for you. Make your answer to those who question you be your continual pursuit of God and your unwavering submission to the work He is doing in you. The process is personal and is between you and God.

At the time others questioned my sacrifices, I did not fully understand what was happening, so there was no way I would be successful in communicating it to others. Attempting to defend what God is doing against others' opinions will delay your becoming. Do what pleases God! Go forth. Run-on. Do not explain: BECOME!

Affirmation

"My peace rests in God, not in the opinions of men."

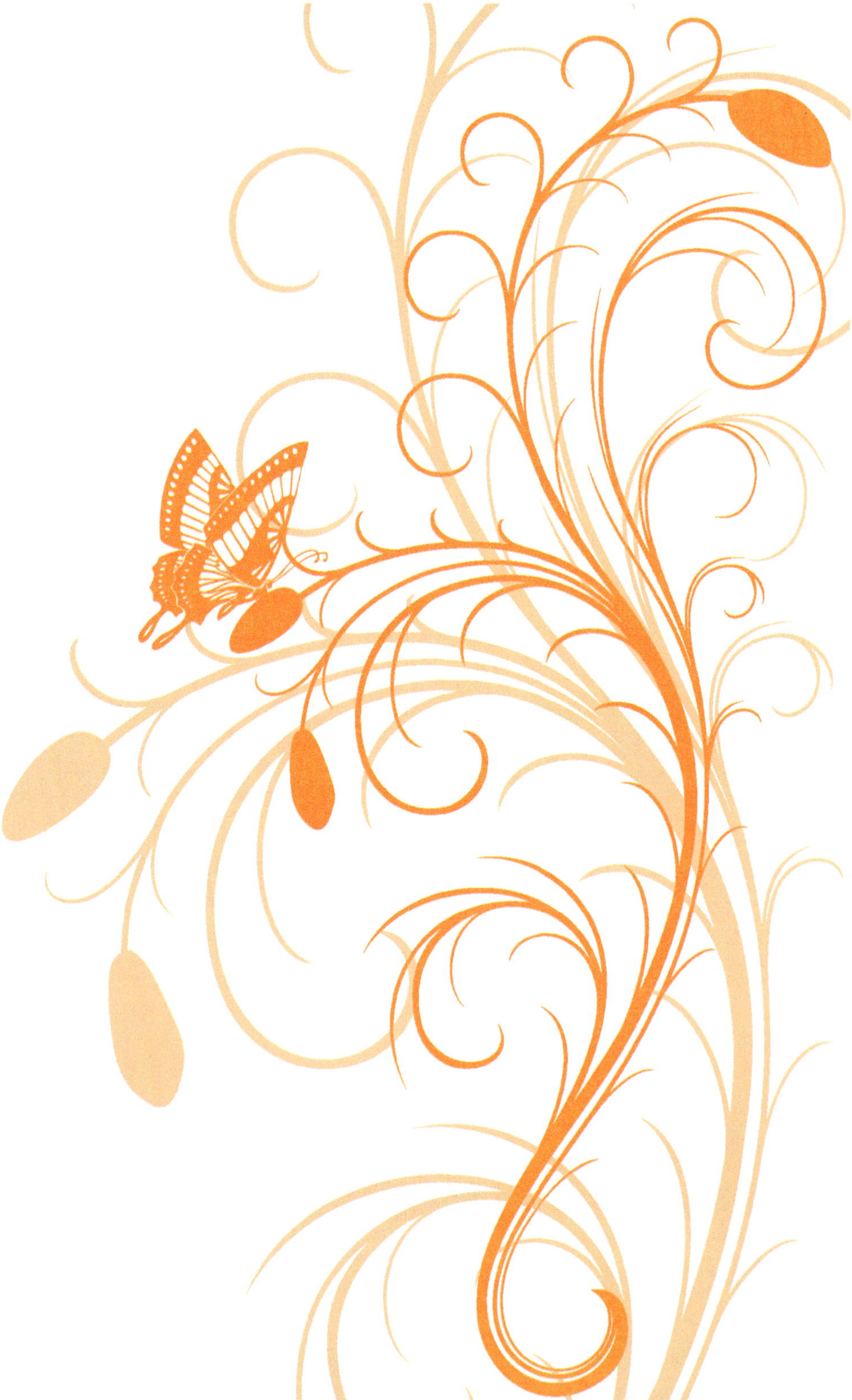

Rejoice

> *A merry heart doeth good like a medicine: but a broken spirit drieth the bones.* PROVERBS 17:22 KJV

You always hear about generational curses, but what about generational blessings. My family is hilarious! When we get together, there are endless family stories. Throughout the generations, we have been blessed with humor and unmatched wit. What I love most about our family gatherings is the unending laughter. Now, we may have heard the family stories told in as many versions as there are books in the bible, yet we laugh at them every time.

We love to have a good time. I appreciate having that family time to lay aside any differences and enjoy each other's presence. Life is demanding enough, so having something to laugh at and someone to laugh with makes the load a little lighter.

The Bible reminds us of the strength found in taking joy in the Lord. We should be overcome with joy when we think of our great salvation. Reflecting on the goodness of God should spark our souls. The assurance of knowing we are not alone, that we have a friend and an advocate who is fighting for our good is reason to be merry.

I marvel at how those who are not in a relationship with God go about life freer than some of His sons and daughters. If anyone should be walking around laughing, singing, skipping, and rejoicing, it should be those who belong to the household of faith!

We have the victory! Regardless of any present sufferings, we are enduring, we will triumph. Christ defeated death and the grave. Even when the saints die, they win, because they will be present with the Lord.

We have endless promises that God is always with us. He is protecting, providing, leading, directing, and speaking to us. Our relentless joy is knowing we have access to uninterrupted fellowship with our Creator. Because of Christ, we can walk and talk with God as Adam did in the garden; we can get as close to Him as we desire. Yes, life gets hard, but we have to remember we are only passing through, fulfilling our assignment. This world is not the end for those who believe in the Lord Jesus Christ.

Enjoy what God has given you in your family, friends, careers, and ministries. Make rejoicing a lifestyle. It is okay to laugh and enjoy what we have been given, for Christ came to give us life more abundantly. Rejoicing is a command! It is a sign of faith in our Father because we have chosen to take our rest in Him. To rejoice is an act of faith that we trust God to work out everything for our good. Regardless of any present sufferings, you are enduring, delight in Him.

Affirmation

"LORD, I choose to rejoice and delight in You."

Be Selfish

> *Beloved, I pray that you may prosper in all things and be in health, just as your soul prospers.* 3 JOHN 2 NKJV

I read an actress' book on her journey to experiencing a more purposeful life. In her quest, she first examined her life and behaviors. She confessed to learning the art of settling for less by observing her mother settling for less. She wrote that her mother did not think she deserved what was good. She had become content with accepting whatever was in front of her without complaint. The actress realized that this in her own life had led to toxic patterns so she resolved to do life differently!

I remember eating dessert, my son asked for some and I emphatically responded, "NO!" I still laugh, picturing the look on my baby's face to his mommy saying no. It was a first for us both. He was shocked because I never told my children no to food and truth be told, I shocked myself! I cannot recall the treat, but it was a pivotal moment for me, putting me first.

The dessert was good and I wanted all of it! That day was a proud mommy moment for me because I did not respond the way the guilt-ridden, fear of rejection version of me would have in that situation. Though he had eaten all of his own, I still would have given him mine. For years I operated under a false sense of self-sacrificing, doing and saying what I did not want to so others would be happy. There was no rule demanding I give in to the wishes of others; I had developed toxic patterns of betraying myself to appease others.

During my years of singleness, before a husband or children, I was not a good steward of my time. Knowing I was single, others placed demands on my time and I willingly obliged. It did not matter if it was family, my job, or the ministry, I had made no plans for my time. In those moments, I had every right to say no as forcefully as I did about giving up my dessert that day, but I had not yet matured into the woman who would unapologetically say no and mean it! But I am today! You too have permission to choose yourself. IT IS OK TO BE SELFISH FOR A SEASON! It is perfectly fine to give yourself permission to intentionally cut off people, places, and things and invest in yourself.

You owe it to yourself to examine your life and take inventory of any toxic people-pleasing patterns. Many men and women will exhaust themselves for others and then settle for less when it concerns them, neglecting the opportunity to give the same effort to the wellness of their own body, soul, and spirit. How is God being glorified if you are not nourishing yourself? Invest time in making yourself a priority. No longer unselfishly serve others while neglecting how God desires to refresh and establish you.

I remember making a list of the top ten things of importance to me and reality hit when I noticed I did not make my list! My children were there, family, and ministry made the top five. I questioned how would they be truly blessed if the vessel pouring into them, me, has holes? Being selfish for a season is wise because investing in you is still investing in others. Once you have been restored, you will be better equipped to offer your family, friends, and those you are called to influence a healthier, refined, and more attentive you.

Affirmation

"God is good to me therefore I am good to me."

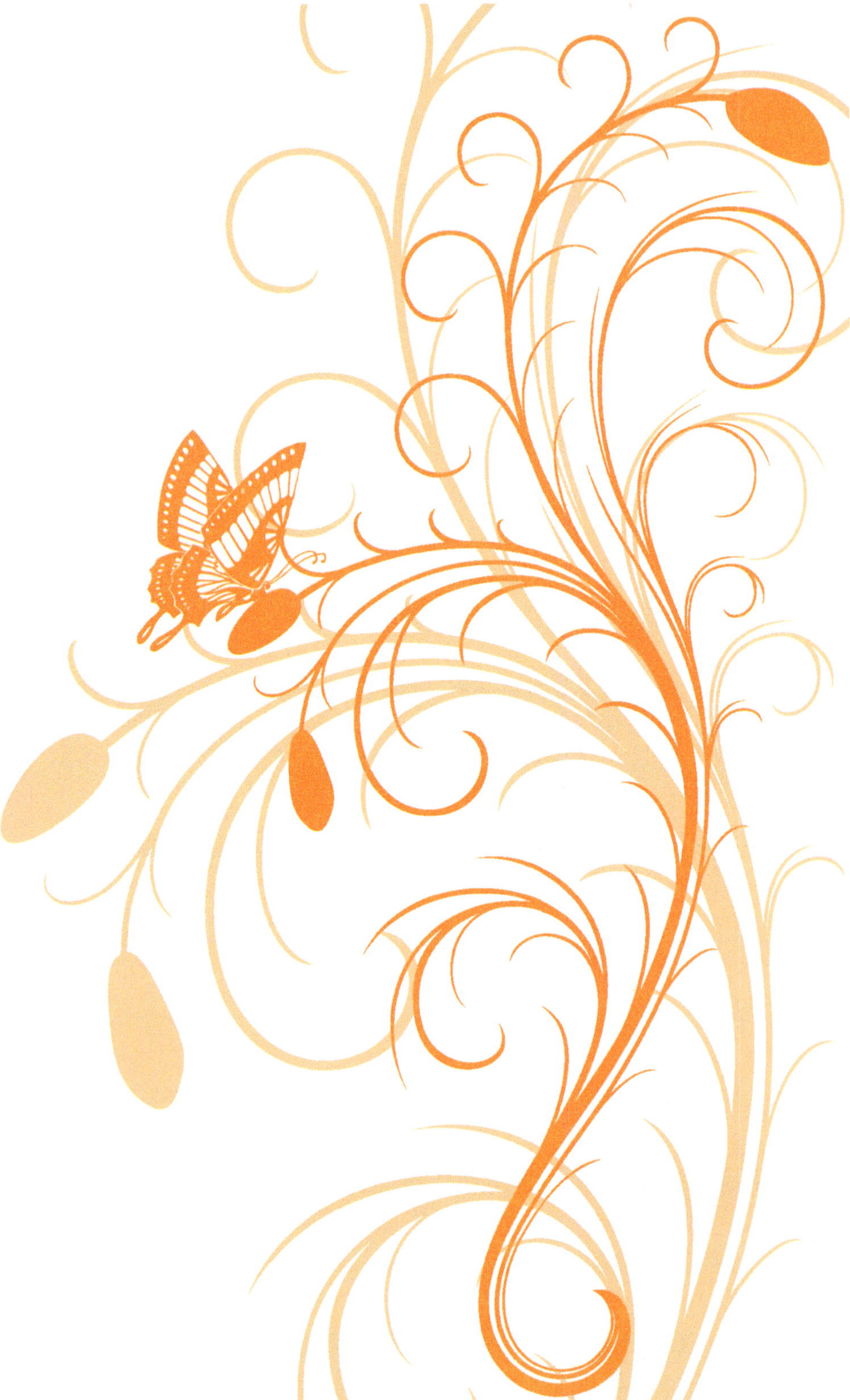

What Is In My Hand

> *And the LORD said unto him, What is that in thine hand? And he said, A rod. EXODUS 4:2 KJV*

The Israelites were God's people. When He heard their cries for deliverance, God remembered the covenant He made with Abraham and vowed to send in a deliverer. Moses was shepherding his father-in-law's flock when he became captivated by a bush that was on fire but not being consumed. God called Moses closer to see the great sight and it was at that moment He commissioned Moses as the deliverer who would bring His people out of Egypt.

Moses's immediate response was to question his identity "who am I that I should go unto Pharaoh and that I should bring forth the children of Israel out of Egypt?" God assured Moses He would be with him. Tell them, "I AM has sent me unto you." Moses was unsure of his qualifications for the assignment, but God had full confidence in his ability to accomplish it. God told Moses exactly what to say and how the people would obey, yet Moses remains unconvinced. God said to him, "what is that in your hand" and Moses replied, "A rod." God commanded Moses to cast it on the ground, and immediately it became the serpent. That one act was only the beginning of the miracles God would perform with what Moses already had in possession.

What is in your hand? What has God given you that you have yet to use to its fullest capabilities? Our Heavenly Father has gifted you with what you need to overcome. There is no need to look upon others with jealousy or contempt for what is in their hand, but the time is ripe to begin to nurture what you have been given.

Living intentionally is capitalizing on what you have. In Matthew 25, the parable of the talents beautifully captures what it means to use what you have.

Again, what is in YOUR HAND! If someone has the same gift or is doing what it is you desire to do, so what! No one can be you better than you can. Work what you know you have been given, perfect it, and master it. Find books, teachings, podcasts, workshops, any available resource, and desire to do and be better.

Invest in you. The servants who took what was given and presented it back to the master with interest were regarded as good and faithful servants and were rewarded more. Your desire should be to hear "well done, my good and faithful servant" because you have shown God can He can trust you to take that which He has blessed you with and make it better and use it to be a blessing to others.

What gift(s) have you been given to advance the kingdom of God? How will you leave your mark here on earth? When you leave this earth there should be evidence that you were not only here because you made an impact! As Moses responded in obedience to God's commands, the rod in his hand, which was an ordinary walking stick, performed extraordinary acts under the power and influence of the Almighty God.

Affirmation

"I am using all of my gifts and talents for God's glory."

Chosen

> *But ye are a chosen generation, a royal priesthood, an holy nation, a peculiar people: that ye should shew forth the praises of him who hath called you out of darkness into his marvelous light. 1 PETER 2:9 KJV*

For years I was not kind to Adecia. I did not treat myself well. Before I was able to come into myself and love who I was, a root of self-rejection had already begun because according to others I was too tall, my voice was too deeper and I was too skinny among other harmful insults. My response was to attribute my overall worth to the negative views of others. I was tall and skinny with a deep voice so those things were facts, but they were not TRUTH! There was so much more to me that they were ignorant to.

Fast forward and I am introduced to Christ, and I begin to hear the truth, which was all the wonderful things God said about me. They sounded great, and I wanted to believe them, but in my mind, I pondered "but I am also…" It was challenging to accept what I heard but a seed was planted in me to want to hear more! I began to consume every recording and book in my aunt's library. In Romans 12:3, we are cautioned not to think more highly of ourselves than we ought to but please do not misinterpret that. It does not mean you are to think less of yourself yet to remain sober in your thinking.

There has to be a dismantling of any negative thoughts. Your identity should be rooted in what the word of God says. You must come into agreement with how great you truly are. When you think soberly, you acknowledge God as the source of all you are. Through His grace bestowed upon you. God has made you elect through His grace bestowed upon you. That manner of thinking honors God.

I love nature, and occasionally I will drive around to behold the handiwork of God. What resonates with me is that God did not minimize His greatness. All creation is filled with His marvelousness. There is no doubt that He alone is God! So why would you minimize who you are? There is nothing wrong with confessing "yes I am chosen," "yes I am royal," "yes I am gifted and anointed," and "yes, the hand of God is on me." Acknowledge who you are then give God the glory.

It does not make you puffed up or make you better than the next person. Too many believers are walking around not exercising the power that is rightfully theirs as joint-heirs with Christ because they have minimized who they truly are in Him. Jesus knew exactly who He was. He was confident in His identity as the Son whom the Father was well pleased with. He did not boast in it rather He walked in humility as He taught and worked miracles. His actions proved He was the Chosen One.

God is with you; you are equipped and empowered for every assignment He has called you to. God gets no glory out of me or you if we think we are anything less than chosen, royal, holy, and His beloved. We are sons and daughters of The King, seated with Christ in heavenly places, redeemed from sin and shame. As members of God's royal family, we are the salt of the earth and the light of the world. We are God's masterpieces, timeless and unique, created in love.

Affirmation

"I am complete in Christ!"

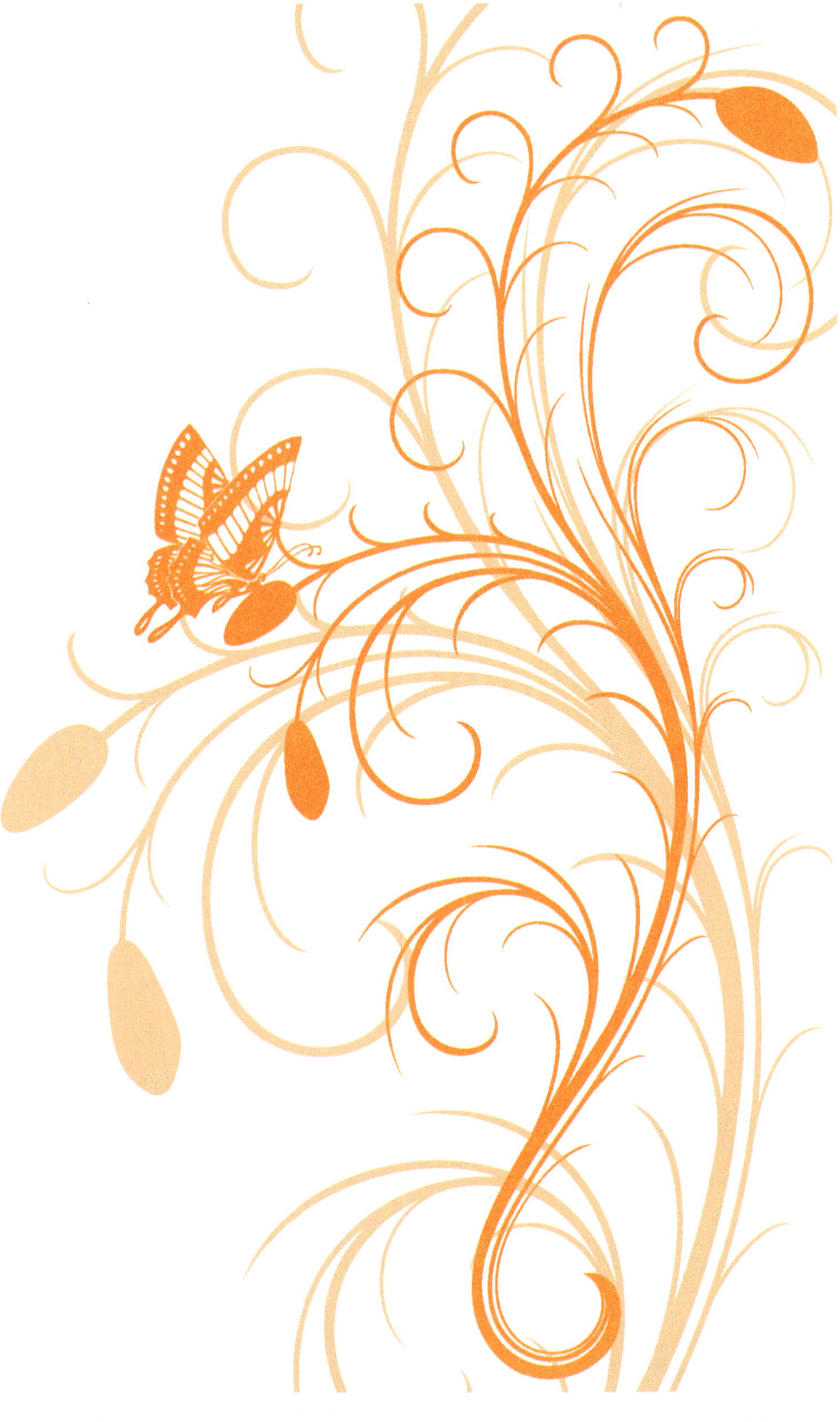

God Has Not Changed His Mind About Me

For the gifts and calling of God are without repentance.
ROMANS 11:29 KJV

In the book of Genesis, God spoke to Abraham and established a covenant with him. God promised to make him a great nation and to make his name great. Abraham questioned how this would be so when he did not have an heir in his household, but God assured him he would have an heir, and despite his age, his heir would come from his own body.

Abram was 75 years old at the time God spoke this to him. Instead of trusting God and waiting on the promise, his wife Sarah gave her handmaiden to Abraham to give them an heir.

Impatient with God's timing, they interfered, trying to force the promise to happen in their timing. In His mercy, God still blessed the handmaiden's son Ishmael, but he reminded Abraham Ishmael was not the heir through whom God would begin His holy nation.

As promised, in their old age, Abraham and Sarah gave birth to Isaac, the one through whom God would establish His covenant! Yes, they disobeyed God, but it did not change what God had already intended for Abraham. God is a promise keeper and He is faithful to His word.

As foolish as this seems, this is not uncommon behavior. Throughout scripture and in our lifetime, many have tried to help God out by doing things our way without seeking Him. I too have gotten a promise and, in "my" wisdom, attempted to create Adecia's version of what God had spoken without receiving the strategy from Him. I unwisely acted on God's behalf and then dared to expect Him to bless what "my" hands had created!

I did not have the patience to wait on the promise or get the divine plan. God knew the plans He had towards Abraham and how HE would prosper him. Thank God who is rich in mercy because Abraham's and Sarah's wrongdoing did not stop what was destined.

Even if or when we get in God's way, His plans for us do not change. He does not take back our gifts and callings. If we have taken matters into our own hands, it is wise to repent quickly and get back in divine alignment. While my disobedience has caused me to miss many opportunities, Philippians 1:6 reminds us that we can be confident of this that He who began a good work in us is faithful to perform it, He will bring it to pass. Wait on God's timing.

Draw close to God with the expectation to hear what He will say. He knows the way you should go! Trust Him; the promises will come to pass in due season. You cannot rush or influence Him because there is a reason for His timing. Creation testifies to the intentionality of God. He acts on purpose and with purpose! Be still and know that He is sovereign and knows how He desires to live through you.

It is easy to get ahead of God, assuming to know better than He does regarding your life. Even in your disobedience, God has not changed His mind about you. Restoration awaits you! Humbly acknowledge it and then submit to the leading of the Holy Spirit as you are led back on the path of righteousness for His namesake.

Affirmation

"God plans for me are coming to pass."

Rest And Restoration

> *But Martha was cumbered about much serving, and came to him, and said, Lord, dost thou not care that my sister hath left me to serve alone? bid her therefore that she help me. And Jesus answered and said unto her, Martha, Martha, thou art careful and troubled about many things: but one thing is needful: and Mary hath chosen that good part, which shall not be taken away from her.*
>
> LUKE 10: 40-42 KJV

Mary, Martha, and their brother Lazarus were friends of Jesus, so it was only fitting that as He passed through their village, Jesus would be welcomed into their home. Martha received Jesus into her home but became distracted serving her guests. If you have ever hosted guests, it is easy to become distracted by guaranteeing the guest has the best experience while unintentionally neglecting the guest. I can relate to Martha, and so may you.

At some point, while serving, she became overwhelmed with all she was doing and looked for her sister Mary to assist her, and she found Mary sitting at the feet of Jesus. Martha was upset and angrily approached Jesus because she felt He did not care that she was left to serve alone. Mary was not just sitting at the feet of any random guest. There may have still been guests to serve and dishes to wash, but Jesus was in the house! There was no person or task more important.

Jesus expressed to Martha that she was worried about too many things, and Mary had chosen what was needed and best for the moment, which was to sit at His feet. In Motorsports, drivers pull into the pit area to refuel, change tires, or have repairs done. Pit stops are critical for the safety of the driver and the car. The skill and timeliness of the crew to fix issues can determine if a race is won or lost.

Along this journey, we must take pit stops for daily maintenance. It is not an option but a necessity! Our survival demands refueling to obtain optimal performance. Life pulls on each of us whether you are working in the ministry, serving your families and friends, and job or business demands. Those obligations may leave very little time for the one thing that is needed, which is connecting to The One who is the source of all of those blessings. Those pit stops won't just happen; we have to intentionally seek God and choose the good part as Mary did.

The good part that Jesus honored requires you to have a consistent devotional time where you daily commune with God. I have to schedule mine early in the morning because once my children are awake, it may be hours before I have alone time! If I have not made time for my morning devotion, it is more difficult to find that uninterrupted time because of all my other responsibilities.

Resting at Jesus' feet is acknowledging Him as the source of your strength. It is the realization that He empowers you to handle what is before us. Resting also allows you to reset and prioritize the demands of life. Resting allows you to hear instructions on what matters and is worthy of your attention. After you have rested, He stores you, and now you come out of your much-needed pit stop refreshed, revived, renewed, and ready for the day.

Our relationship with God is and should be your most important relationship. He gives you the strength, wisdom, and grace needed to pour into your other relationships. Always keep Him first by committing to do the needful part.

Affirmation

"I find rest and I am restored at the feet of Jesus."

Love On Purpose

> *By this shall all men know that ye are my disciples, if you have love one for another.* JOHN 13:35 KJV

Jesus knew His time had come, and He would soon be going back to the Father. After announcing His approaching departure to the disciples, He left them with a new commandment "Love one another. As I have loved you, so you must love one another." Jesus said that by doing this, all men would know they were His disciples by their love for one another. For those called by God, love is not an option. God expects you to love. It is written how we can say we love God whom we have not seen and cannot love our brothers and sisters whom we have seen.

Why must you choose to love? For God so loved the world that He gave us Jesus. Love was God's motivation in blessing us with His Son and in the end eternal life. Likewise, love should be the motivating factor driving the work we do. Why must you choose to love? Whatever God has called you to do involves people. The kingdom of God is the representation of a family working together for the greater good of all. Jesus said He and the father are one and it is the standard set for all in the kingdom of God.

Jesus commanded us to love our neighbor as we love ourselves. There is an expectancy that we are loving ourselves first, so we know how to give it to others. This is critical and cannot be overlooked. Choosing to love is not only what we do for others, but it is also seeking what is in our own best interest. We have to be good to ourselves.

Love costs and it may hurt. Ask Jesus! Yet it is a commandment. Choosing to love is not always easy but God will help you to love. It is human nature when you are hurt to withdraw from the person or thing causing the hurt. We can effortlessly create walls to block out the pain and suffering.

Self-preservation is natural. To desire to protect yourself is healthy but you cannot remain behind the wall. Your calling will call you onward. Jesus was the perfect example of keeping your eye on what is set before you despite the hardships that come along with the pursuit.

God is love! God's grace, giving us what we do not deserve is His love in action. God's mercy, not giving us what we do deserve is also love His love in action and he does not expect any less for those who are His. The reason you are who you are and able to accomplish what you have is because of the love of God.

When there is an appreciation of God's love for us in light of our shortcomings, it can empower us to love those we may deem unlovable. God saw beyond our faults and He expects us to have His heart. The world will indeed know we are God's by how we LOVE. I thank God we have the Holy Spirit who helps us to love.

Purposely employ these tools of love: Hug, Smile, Encourage, Motivate, Challenge, Comfort, Admonish, Kiss, Inspire, and Forgive! Remain a willing and available vessel of love so there are no limits on how God can use you.

Love Yourself. Love God. Love His People. Love Your Assignment.

Affirmation

"I choose to love."

Divine Connections

And it happened, when Elizabeth heard the greeting of Mary, that the babe leaped in her womb; and Elizabeth was filled with the Holy Spirit. Then she spoke out with a loud voice and said, "Blessed are you among women, and blessed is the fruit of your womb!
LUKE 1: 41-42 KJV

Throughout scripture, you will find divine relationships. God often brought together those whose purposes were connected. Jonathan, King Saul's son loved David and made a covenant with him. Ruth remained loyal to her widowed mother-in-law Naomi and returned with her to Bethlehem. Aaron was an invaluable asset to Moses and often spoke to the people on his brother's behalf. Elisha was Prophet Elijah's protégé and asked and inherited a double portion of Elijah's spirit after he was taken up. God connects His people to those who will help them come into the fullness of what they are chosen to be.

In Luke Chapter 1, Elizabeth was pregnant with John the Baptist and her cousin Mary was pregnant with Jesus. John the Baptist would grow up to be the voice crying out to the people preparing the way for Jesus. When Elizabeth heard the voice of Mary, it is written he leaped in her womb and she was filled with the Holy Spirit. Jesus' and John the Baptist's divine connection was a fulfillment of Isaiah's prophecy of the voice of a man who would prepare the way for the Lord.

Like those mentioned, you too are someone's divine connection! Someone is waiting on what is in you to make their dreams a reality. Imagine God has ordained for you to be connected to someone, and together the two of you will create life-changing experiences for others!

Whether the connection is in your personal life, business, or ministry, you should expect God to connect you to the persons or groups who have been called to help you maximize your calling. Purposely connect with those who have similar passions, grab hold of the vision, and unite in purpose.

Pray and ask the Holy Spirit to reveal those divine relationships. Inviting the Holy Spirit in will help you to weed out the wrong people that the enemy may try to send in your life to sabotage God's plan. Making the right connections adds value to your life. Once the Holy Spirit reveals those relationships, nurture them. Prayerfully ask God for His will to be done through the connection.

In Mary and Elizabeth's story, the hand of God is there orchestrating every scene. In His infinite wisdom, He is weaving all the pieces together as only He could.

I remember as a new believer receiving a prophetic word and being commissioned. My aunt was by my side and she was also commissioned and given the responsibility to pray over me and to assist me in carrying out my assignment. Twenty years later and our relationship is beyond familial because there is a divine purpose attached to our connection.

Recently God has brought others into my life. My connection to them has given me much clarity and language for the season I am now in. Do not alienate yourself from others or assume God wants you to do life on your own. Connect!

Affirmation

"I am grateful for divine relationships."

About the author

Adecia is a proud Mom, Educator, Realtor, Podcaster, and Author. Born and raised in Franklin, Louisiana, she now lives in Ardmore, Alabama with her three children Reginald II, Reighan, and Aden. Writing has always been her outlet when needing to make sense of the world. Creative writing is her first love.

Adecia's natural and spiritual gift is teaching. She completed Master's degree programs in Educational Leadership and Clinical Psychology which she uses as she educates the Body of Christ. She delights in ministering to turn the hearts of the people back to the Father.

She is a member of her church's ministerial staff where she currently serves as the Coordinator of the Intercessory Prayer Ministry.

Made in the USA
Columbia, SC
22 July 2023